Rethinking Stress
in an Age of Ease

Rethinking Stress in an Age of Ease

A Field Manual for Students of all Ages

WILLIAM J. ELENCHIN

Foreword by Jack Smith

RESOURCE *Publications* · Eugene, Oregon

RETHINKING STRESS IN AN AGE OF EASE
A Field Manual for Students of all Ages

Resource Publications
An Imprint of Wipf and Stock Publishers
199 W. 8th Ave., Suite 3
Eugene, OR 97401

www.wipfandstock.com

PAPERBACK ISBN: 978-1-5326-6486-1
HARDCOVER ISBN: 978-1-5326-6487-8
EBOOK ISBN: 978-1-5326-6488-5

Manufactured in the U.S.A.   JANUARY 28, 2019

This book is dedicated to my students. Heck, they are the ones who gave me the idea for writing such a book, which you'll read about in the next section.

College students often get a bad rap in our culture. They can be seen as not working hard enough, consuming too many beers, and living in a bubble that protects them from the real world.

Yet most of these young adults come to university with noble intentions. They want to learn, grow, and develop their potential.

This generation of learners is also living during extraordinary times. On the one hand they have access to the products of technology that would be the envy of every generation that has preceded them. But on the other hand they must learn to navigate a bloated culture that daily pounds them with the message that a life of ease will make them happy. But most of our students know, or at least sense, that such an idea just isn't true.

So they select a major, take classes, rack up demoralizing student loans, and often have their endurance tested by stale professors and death by power point. And all of this is really an act of faith, with a hope for a future of meaning and purpose.

These young adults help me to remember that, in a very real sense, we are all students on a continual search for that same meaning, purpose, and perhaps the occasional cold beer.

Contents

Foreword

So, OUT OF THE blue I get a surprise letter from my dear friend and former colleague, Will, wishing me well and asking me if I might write a foreword to his latest book, a practical guide on managing stress. I should mention it was mid-December with all the attendant hustle and bustle before the holidays, and a few days before my daughters and eight family members would take turns visiting us in Florida for two weeks. Nothing too out of the ordinary there except Will also mentioned his publisher was set to go and I'd likely get a call requesting a rush. Did I mention this was a book on STRESS?!

I first met Will nearly 25 years ago when we began working with youngsters twelve to 18 years old who were adjudicated and sent to our residential treatment facility. You can probably imagine the stress levels of both staff and residents in our building where the youth were enrolled in a fifteen-week program to "turn their lives around." Reading Will's book took me back to those days where we used to share many stories with our clients, help them examine reasons to change, and facilitate personal problem-solving for better behavior management and life choices. Indeed, Will masterfully tells stories and facilitates the reader's critical thinking and personal actions via his use of illustrations, motivations and applications throughout the book.

Will is certainly well qualified to write such a book not just from our joint work with juvenile delinquents, but because the vast majority of his adult life has been devoted to helping others through his teaching and mentoring in the field of sociology, health, and wellness. He skillfully simplifies the complexity of brain chemistry, human physiology, and a vast array of emotions we're likely to encounter. Will then shares his own expertise by providing a practical, easy-to-read prescriptive guide that truly warrants the handle of "field manual."

Yet another proof of how well Will deals with stress: he actually tried to teach me how to golf. As a recent USN retiree, I was the oldest of the new employees beginning our RTF indoctrination class and accordingly a bit older than Will, about 15-plus years. So Will and his lovely wife decided my wife and I should learn how to hit the links. Any of you golfers out there can easily identify with what stressors we may have put the Elenchins through. But in a style all his own, Will took up the challenge without looking back. He mentored us just as easily as he worked with troubled youth, with enthusiasm, determination, and solid, down-to-earth knowledge. Will has put that same youthful energy sharing his expertise into his practical guide for dealing with life's challenges without resorting to medicalization or material fixes . . . at least until seeking a health professional is warranted.

As a retired psychotherapist, I'm honored to write this brief foreword and I heartily endorse Will's holistic approach to wellbeing. I suppose I should clarify how that stressful holiday deadline I alluded to at the beginning turned out just fine as a more flexible schedule allowed me a relaxed and enjoyable read of Will's latest book. He has provided a wonderful resource for his own (stressed) college students and anyone else who could benefit from some easy-to-absorb tips on managing one's biopsychosocial wellness. Don't just read this "manual"—Live it.

JACK SMITH,
Mindfully living in Florida.

Preface

THIS BOOK IS ABOUT a word many of us think about most days. "Stress."

We come across this word regularly when we read news accounts, think about our own hectic lives, or hear others talk about being "stressed out." However, it's likely that we've never really considered what this term actually means.

My motivation for this writing project has been to help many of my college students who often chat with me about how stressed they are. These conversations have led me to wonder why people perceive life situations so differently. Why do some enjoy public speaking while others have fear of getting up in front of others? How is that one person enjoys heights while elevation fills another with panic?

Work as a college professor is, for the most part, simply a fun job. You get to read about and study topics that you're interested in. Even more so, you're able to teach and discuss those subjects with students. While not every young learner is as interested in every course as his or her instructor, for the most part they have a strong degree of inherent motivation and are in class to learn.

Sociology, the discipline in which I teach, is concerned with exploring how society impacts historical and contemporary life. Some have the misconception that only psychology examines human behavior. However, that's not the case. Sociology plays a key role in discovering the many ways in which our culture influences our lives.

It will come as a surprise to no one that our culture profoundly influences people's lives. This is self-evident. Looking at history we can readily see its impact in every century. From the Spartan civilization of loyalty to the state and military service, to the renaissance period of literature, the arts, and science, to our modern consumer society, culture is a powerful force.

What may be a revelation to some are the many *subtle* ways in which culture seeps into our lives. It's easy to read about the Middle Ages' practice of bleeding as a medical treatment (the practice continued into more modern times . . . the first US president died largely as a result of this treatment) and feel sorry that folks who lived back then weren't as *enlightened* as we are today. Yet with all of our advanced knowledge compared to those who have lived in the past, we can still learn things that we assume are helpful to us but in the long run are harmful.

For example, as a society we've made exponential gains in the availability and affordability of food during the past century. Yet this overabundance has brought with it a dramatic rise in rates of obesity. Statistics from the Centers for Disease and Control and Prevention tell us that 70 percent of US adults are either overweight or obese.[1] Such individuals are at an increased likelihood of suffering a host of physical ailments, including high blood pressure, diabetes, sleep apnea, cancer, and poor body image.

At times I feel especially fortunate in my work, in that I get to teach health-related subjects that are inherently interesting for most people. These include courses on "addictions" and "health and illness." In our addictions course, we look at how our culture feeds the problem even more than we look at the chemistry of chemical dependence. The same holds true for our class on health and illness, where we explore the ways in which consumer messaging can lead to poor health.

Health-related classes tend to interest students because they are applicable to everyone. All of us have a sense of our own well-being, even though we experience health and life differently. And of course while not everyone struggles with addiction, most of us

1. Centers for Disease Control, "Obesity and Overweight," line 2.

arc attached to some behaviors, and all of us go through times of well-being and times of illness. Both of these are complex subjects, with many factors in play that need to be considered.

One key factor in understanding health is not only the role that *stress* plays in our lives, but also pondering what is even meant by this common word we hear thrown about on a regular basis. Rethinking the concept of stress, and ways not to avoid, but embrace it, is what this guidebook is all about.

Introduction

Life is either a daring adventure or nothing at all.

HELEN KELLER (1880–1968)

OVER THE PAST DOZEN years of teaching students about health, perhaps the most common discussion point we hit on is the notion of *stress*, stress both in their lives and in our society. On several occasions, typically near the end of the semester, I'll ask students the question, "if you were interested in reading a book about health, what topic would you put at the top of your list?" More times than not, they answered: *stress*.

Life during college can be very demanding. Personal changes include: moving away from home; leaving parents, caretakers, and siblings; and being assigned a small dorm room to share with, at least initially, a total stranger. Academic challenges range from needing to master difficult course materials to developing good rapport with a variety of professorial personalities. Social trials take the form of making new friends, navigating the college party culture, and developing romantic relationships.

Most students, when thinking the many changes to be confronted when going to college, would summarize them as being *stressful*. And, in a certain sense, they would be right. But in another sense, they would be missing the mark. That's because, for many reasons, the concept of stress has taken on an almost exclusively negative connotation within our culture. We have come to believe that any demands placed upon our minds and bodies are in some way unnatural and to be avoided.

Of course, too much pressure exerted upon anything can cause damage. We wear seat belts and have airbags to protect our bodies from being crushed in an accident. But at the same time the very act of being alive requires effort, whether we are conscious of it or not. Every night we expend energy and burn 500 calories during sleep to fuel our autonomous nervous system, which keeps us breathing and alive.

The word *stress* is ubiquitous. It is simply everywhere and means different things to different people. This concept is used, perhaps primarily, as a general term to describe a cocktail of negative emotions related to feeling overwhelmed, taxed, and exhausted. Most of us apply it to a host of daily experiences:

- Final exam week stresses me out!

- It's very important to avoid stress in your life.

- My job is so stressful!

- I'm stressed out.

- You seem a bit stressed.

- Stress is bad for your health.

- He has a problem dealing with stress.

- Did you know too much stress could cause a heart attack?

- How do you deal with all of that stress?

In writing this book I do not intend to take on the varied meanings and nuances that are often associated with this term. That would be too stressful! In a related manner, this word is also often used as a substitute for anxiety and depression, both of which can be clinical in nature. Meaning there are times when people experience tragic loss and pain that are not only stressful, but go to a level of suffering that is far beyond the daily challenges of navigating life. In such profoundly difficult circumstances, individuals may require expert assistance from professionals in the fields of counseling, medicine, clergy, or related specialties.

I can appreciate the difference between severe kinds of distress from both professional and personal experience. My own involvement in the health field is primarily in behavioral health, having worked for the better part of a decade as a family therapist prior to teaching college. I have certainly worked with individuals who were dealing with behavioral health issues that go far beyond what we could consider "typical" life challenges. The most compelling, for me, were children who struggled with organic conditions, such as autism, as well as those who were tragically abused at an early age.

I've also experienced on a personal level the difference between living with daily life pressures and severe distress. Shortly after turning 50 years of age I experienced a very strange and extremely debilitating illness called Post-Viral Syndrome (PVS). Other names are also given to this syndrome because it is just that, a *syndrome*. Syndromes are health conditions that typically consist of clusters of symptoms that present in a way that eludes a straightforward classification or diagnosis. My PVS symptoms were very much like the most intense flu I've ever experienced that lasted for two full years, which made daily life virtually unmanageable.

It took several months and consultations with four physicians to arrive at my diagnosis. Part of the difficulty of living with this condition was its very strange nature. Having taught a course on "health and illness" ten years before becoming ill, we had covered the nature of syndromes as described in our textbook and how they are often very painful to live with. Even biological tests often fail to detect any significant evidence that anything is wrong in many of these conditions. Such was my case. Basically I had a complete medical work-up done which showed overall good heath, but I felt terribly ill for years. I consider myself most fortunate to have made a full recovery, since many who struggle with this illness take much longer to recover, and related conditions can last a lifetime.

One of the lessons I've learned from this challenging time is the mistaken way in which our culture often portrays illness as being one-dimensional. We are either healthy or unhealthy, as evidenced by what our test results indicates.

Health must be seen along the line of a continuum. None of us are completely "healthy" or not. Everyone has her or his challenges from time to time. They may take the form of physical, mental, spiritual, emotional, or relational. But the *perfect* doesn't exist, at least outside of popular culture.

The purpose of this book is twofold. The first is to dispel the widely-held notion that *stress* in life is inherently a bad thing. The second is to suggest different ways of looking at this concept, which can offer an alternative approach to engaging with the challenges that are natural to life.

As the title suggests, this book takes a *new* look at stress from a sociological and holistic perspective. Sociology, like its sister social science of psychology, is a vast field. However, one of the central focus points in sociology is uncovering meaning behind the symbols that we often take for granted. And the most important of all symbols is language.

In addition, while it is self-evident that culture plays a powerful role in shaping our experience of life, there are times when what we think is settled, simply isn't the case. To say that another way, there are times when we need to 'unlearn' things. The great Christian apologist G. K. Chesterton (1874–1936) recognized the importance of this when writing, "Without education, we are in a horrible and deadly danger of taking educated people seriously."[2]

This is also written not so much as a traditional textbook, but more like a field manual. Part of my inspiration for writing the book is from working with college students and our discussions about stress in many of my classes on campus. The word "campus" is from the Latin and literally means "field," meaning an expansive outside surrounding. So a field manual can also mean a "campus manual." I also like the feel and simplicity of the field manual format. After I graduated from college I spent a total of eight years in the army. Most of the publications we used came in the form of

2. Chesterton, *More Quotable Chesterton*, 139.

field manuals, which are short and to-the-point handbooks covering a variety of military tasks.

This is also not meant to be an exhaustive work on stress, but a reference guide that clarifies key central concepts. The topic of stress has captivated our society. There are hundreds of books written about "dealing with stress," in addition to literally countless academic journal articles dedicated to this topic. This is a back-to-basics kind of thing . . . for "stressed" people the simpler the better, as my daughter likes to say!

This book is organized in a way that isn't necessarily linear. It's not meant to be a textbook, more of a manual of what stress is, is not, and ways to better approach life's challenges. I would invite you to flip to whichever section seems to interest you.

1

Brief History of
the Discovery of Stress

IT'S BEEN JUST OVER 100 years since Harvard physiologist Walter Cannon uncovered the ways we respond to the many demands life makes upon us, or what would later become known as *stress.* Cannon recognized that the human body, when in an undisturbed state, maintains a stable level of functioning. He called the experience of being physically at ease *homeostasis,* which means "steady state." To say that another way, homeostasis refers to the relaxed state of being we experience when undisturbed.

Cannon also recognized that when we are presented with various challenges, especially those we perceive as a threat to our very existence, our bodies automatically respond. Physiologically speaking, our sympathetic nervous system is activated, so that we are energized to deal with whatever threatens us.[1]

Our sympathetic nervous system is part of the autonomic nervous system. It is termed *autonomic* because we do not consciously or intentionally control it. Also, part of the autonomic nervous system is the parasympathetic nervous system, known

1. Cannon, *Bodily Changes in Pain, Hunger, Fear, and Rage,* 24–25.

as the "rest and digest" system, since it controls bodily functions when the mind and body are at ease.

In 1915, Cannon famously coined the phrase *fight or flight* to refer to animals' (including humans) innate response to either engage with or flee from a real or perceived threat. When we sense harm, our sympathetic nervous system is activated. This is a natural and evolutionary process directly related to our survival

The sympathetic and parasympathetic essentially perform opposite functions. The sympathetic system prepares us for action, while the parasympathetic system regulates our normal bodily functions. Some of the natural reactions that occur when our sympathetic system is activated include:

- Quickening heart rate

- Rapid breathing

- Slowing of digestion

- Widening of pupils

- Loss of peripheral vision (tunnel vision)

These physical responses serve one singular purpose—to maximize our decision-making, speed, and strength in anticipation of battle or escape.

Cannon's work laid the foundation for medical doctor and Austrian-born Hans Selye, who is credited with developing our modern notion of *stress*. Prior to this time, most people were not aware of their "stress" level as we so often hear about today, because the concept of "stress" was not yet developed.

In 1926, Selye was a 19-year-old sophomore college student studying at the University of Prague when he experienced an epiphany about how the body responds to illness. His instructor, Professor von Jaksch, a noted hematologist (a doctor who specializes in the diagnosis and treatment of blood related disease), was teaching students how to diagnose illnesses based on patient symptoms.

To demonstrate the power of medical knowledge to Selye and his fellow students von Jaksch examined five patients who were suffering with unrelated ailments, and correctly identified each illness based upon their symptoms. Selye was astonished by the accuracy of the diagnoses. In addition, he was also struck at how each of the five people had the same general appearance, in that they looked ill, or what he termed "the syndrome of just being sick".[2]

One doesn't need to be a trained medical doctor to know that when people feel ill, a majority of the time they also look sick. One usually goes with the other. Yet this rather evident observation caught Selye's attention. For, in his mind, this is when he first connects the general appearance of being sick with stress. Selye writes, "This may seem ridiculously childish and self-evident, but it was because I wondered about the obvious that the concept of "stress" was born in my mind."[3]

Selye pursued this line of thinking with his professor but was essentially mocked for making such elemental and obvious statements. He would continue his medical studies for another ten years before more substantially diving into the study of stress. His more advanced work began in 1936, just a few years after moving to Canada. He conducted initial research, primarily on rats, by manipulating their living environment (putting them on a treadmill, exposing them to the elements by placing them outside in winter, injecting them with toxins) in order to place them under stress so that he could observe their physical reactions.[4]

In his research Selye eventually arrived at the discovery of the chemical reactions that can occur in the body when under duress, or what he termed "stress hormones."[5] Among these include:

- ACTH (adrenocorticotropic hormone)—A hormone secreted by the pituitary gland.

- Adrenalin/Epinephrine—A hormone and neurotransmitter

2. Selye, *Stress of My Life*, 56.
3. Selye, *Stress of My Life*, 56.
4. Selye, *Stress of My Life*, 63.
5. Selye, *Stress of My Life*, 63–64.

- Corticoids—A class of hormones produced in the adrenal cortex

- CRF—A hormone produced by nerve cells

These stress hormones are created by the body as needed, to enable animals and humans to face the many challenges and difficulties in life.

A PENDULUM FOR YOUR THOUGHT

Selye uncovered the physiological reactions our bodies undergo when under duress. However, in our lives, the pendulum swings both ways, meaning that it is part of our human nature to experience times of difficulty. But it is also natural for everyone to have times of accomplishment, fun, and pleasure. These positive experiences also move us out of a state of homeostasis and make demands upon body and nervous system. In fact, they make virtually the same demands as when negative things happen.

Selye called these similar reactions to the ups and downs in life the "feature of *nonspecifity*."[6] "Nonspecifity" means that the body produces chemicals which cause our heart rate to increase, eyes to dilate, breathing rate to go up, and blood pressure to rise for both pain *and* pleasure.

As Selye writes, "We can now provide concrete evidence that great joy can produce the same nonspecific biochemical changes in the body as intense pain." He pointed out that this principle of nonspecifity could and should be used beyond the medical field in our understanding of health, adding, "Once you have understood this you have grasped the very essence of the stress concept as applied to medicine, psychology, sociology or any other field."[7]

At a basic level, stress is not necessarily good or bad but simply a physiological response to being alive. We can readily see this when looking at two individuals who see an activity, such as public speaking, differently. One has tremendous anxiety at the very

6. Selye, *Stress of My Life*, 67.
7. Selye, *Stress of My Life*, 67.

thought of getting up in front of an audience. Another searches out such occasions because they enjoy talking to people. Selye understood how personal and situational factors come into play, as his own definition of stress is nothing more than "the non-specific response of the body to any demand for change."[8]

Selye also conceptualized stress as having one of four effects upon the body. Good stress, which he termed "eustress," is the type of excitement we feel when we enjoy an engaging activity, such as sports or laughter. He identified bad stress as distress, which we experience when we feel physically ill or sad at the loss a loved one. The other two variations he termed overstressed and understressed (what he called "hyper" and "hypo-stress" respectively) and refer simply to having too many demands placed upon us at school, work or home, or too little activity that results in feeling bored or adrift in life.

Part of Selye's reasoning for identifying these four variations of stress was to prescribe as much eustress as possible in our lives, and to minimize to the extent possible the remaining three elements. Selye, the "Father of stress" made the concept of stress part of our collective conscious. He didn't intend his work to lead to the "all stress is bad" type of cultural mentality that is common today, but that has been the result. By his call to maximize pleasurable life experiences and minimize discomfort he, no doubt unintentionally, advanced an unrealistic view of health in our culture.

SOMETIMES THE DRAGON WINS

Now and again we all see images that pack a punch! That epitomizes the proverbial "a picture is worth a thousand words" sentiment. I recall seeing such a drawing some time ago when in my early twenties. The image depicted was of a very large dragon, sitting on a field of grass with a satisfied smirk, and using a toothpick as if having just finished a good meal. Also in the drawing were the scattered breastplate, helmet, and sword of the knight (the dragon

---

8. Selye, *Stress of My Life*, 63.

was using the lance for a toothpick) who had just lost the battle. The caption at the bottom of the image read *Sometimes the Dragon Wins*.

No one *wants* to suffer. We would all like to live each day of our lives in perfect health and happiness and experience a kind of "heaven on earth." But it's obvious to recognize that such a notion breaks with reality. Every life is full of its share of ups and downs, good times and bad times. In fact, to live with the belief that we can escape difficult experiences is not only unrealistic, but is delusional, and *sets us up* for suffering.

Living with expectations of constant pleasure means that we experience *shock* when we fall ill, argue with a friend, fail at school or work, or things generally don't go our way. We fall into a mindset that something must be wrong with us, because suffering is always a *bad* thing. More to the point is that this notion is powerfully reinforced in our consumer culture, which promises to deliver happiness through any number of products, pleasures, and distractions.

It's both important and fascinating to note that Selye (at age 71 and writing one of his last books) himself recognized how the notion of stress being *bad* had become embedded into our collective consciousness. He noted that "Contrary to widespread public opinion, stress is not synonymous with nervous depression, tension, fatigue or discouragement."[9] He goes on to make the point that distressing situations can lead to a host of psychological and physical ailments in "certain individuals," but that life's challenges, or what Selye terms *disturbances*, are not stress.

Seyle makes a profoundly key point which has been lost in our society. That point is that stress is a *good* and a *natural* part of life. Without stress, we die. He writes:

> You *should not and cannot avoid stress,* because to eliminate it completely would mean to destroy life itself. If you make no demands upon your body, you are dead.[10]

9. Selye, *Stress of My Life*, 91.
10. Selye, *Stress of My Life*, 91.

"If you make no demands upon your body, you are dead." These are powerful words worth repeating. Like a cold shower, they help us wake to reality. All of our lives, from the moment we're born until the day we die, demands are made upon our body, mind, and soul. Stress is not a phenomenon that occasionally makes its presence known when we have a bad day. Stress is a normal part of living.

The stress that Selye "discovered" is, at its core, our body's natural way of empowering us to live our lives. We have all experienced this reaction at different times and in various ways. Like everyone else I've experienced this on several occasions, but one recollection stands above the rest.

One of the most memorable for me occurred five years ago, when I was taking my then 16-year-old son to a doctor's appointment to evaluate an injury. He had suffered a broken bone in his wrist the prior week playing in a high school football game. We live in a rural town and our doctor's office is 20 miles from our home. On the way out of town, just ahead of me was a car traveling at the posted speed limit. During the drive my son and I were relaxed and chatting about those things typical of father-son chats when I saw clearly that the car ahead of me signaled the intent to turn to their left. Automatically I applied foot pressure to my break when, in a literal instant, my pedal went directly to the floor. I recall looking down in disbelief, then right back up at the anticipation of the crash that was about to ensue.

I remember saying to my son "hold on" as we were about to crash. Instinctively I veered to my right between the road and the wood line, barely avoiding the collision, then swerving back to the road before applying my emergency break and coming to a stop. The stench of the emergency break is distinctive, but more so I remember being unbelievably grateful that no one was injured. And to this day I'm most thankful that we have this mechanism built right into our DNA.

The stress response is universal and natural. We all experience it on a regular basis. While we can see it most acutely during dramatic events, it occurs at various levels over each and every day. But what is commonly referred to as this negative condition of "stress" is simply our mind and bodies gearing us up to engage with life.

2

Stress in the Age of Ease

A Perfect Storm

IT IS ONLY DURING the recent past that, as a society, we've begun to perceive much of normal life experiences as being unusually negative. We enjoy longer and exponentially more materially comfortable lives than when our parents and grandparents were our ages. Throughout virtually all of history, life expectancy hovered right around 40 years of age. In the United States it was not until roughly 100 years ago that the average life expectancy began to rise above 40, reaching the current level of 80 years of age.

Yet it is ironic that as our life expectancy and standard of living has risen, so have our perceived levels of stress. We've seen a comparable paradox play out during this past half-century when we consider our physical health. Since the 1970s there's been a dramatic rise in chronic health conditions, such as diabetes, heart disease, and stroke, *in spite* of exponential advancement in medical technology. In 1974 medical sociologist John McKinlay employed a classic analogy to describe how many doctors feel when treating their patients:

Sometimes it feels like this. There I am standing by the shore of a swiftly flowing river and I hear the cry of a drowning man. So I jump into the river, put my arms around him, pull him to shore and apply artificial respiration. Just when he begins to breathe, there is another cry for help. So I jump into the river, reach him, pull him to shore apply artificial respiration, and then just as he begins to breathe, another cry for help. So back in the river again, reaching, pulling, applying, breathing, and then another yell. Again and again and again, without end, goes the sequence. You know, I am so busy jumping in, pulling them to shore, applying artificial respiration, that I have *no* time to see who the hell is upstream pushing them all in.[1]

McKinlay settles on the term "manufacturers of illness"[2] to describe corporations and interest groups (tobacco, fast food, social media, etc.) that promote illness-causing behaviors. While McKinlay spoke primarily to physical health, I would suggest there are three key societal dynamics that have emerged in only that past few decades that help explain this same dramatic rise in perceived levels of distress in our current culture. These are the myth of materialism, dominance of the medical model of illness, and medicalization. These seem to have converged at similar moments in just the past 50 years, creating a kind of perfect storm.

THE MYTH OF MATERIALISM

When teaching our health and illness class I use a supplementary text titled *The How of Happiness,* by Sonja Lyubomirsky. I like to use this particular book because it represents one of the first books on well-being written by a research scientist. So, it is data-driven.

Lyubomirsky points out that today, the average person experiences a standard of living that would equal those who lived as

1. McKinlay, "Case for Refocusing Upstream," 502-3.
2. McKinlay, "Case for Refocusing Upstream," 503.

the *richest 5 percent* just 70 years ago.[3] To say that another way, compared to virtually all of human history, we now live like royalty from a materialistic perspective. She uses this data to make the point that materialism not only doesn't lead to contentment, but scientifically speaking, *can't* create a sense of lasting happiness.

Since the days of the "Greatest Generation," we've enjoyed exponential advances in access to food, clothing, transportation, health advancements, communication, and recreation. For the first time in all of human history, we've lived in a time period where the average person lives with material abundance. Most of the consumer goods we enjoy today didn't even exist a few decades ago. A small sample of what are now essentials include:[4]

- 1939—The first computer was built.

- 1947—The transistor was invented, replacing vacuum tubes for radios, television, and computers, now used in almost all electronics.

- 1955—Jonas Salk developed the polio vaccine. Polio was a dreaded disease up until this time, often paralyzing or killing those infected.

- 1955—The first fast-food restaurant chain, McDonald's, opened its first franchise.

- 1958—The microchip was developed, revolutionizing technology in virtually all products that run on electricity.

- 1968—The Internet is developed.

- 1973—The cell phone is invented.

- 1975—The personal computer is invented.

- 1991—The World Wide Web was launched.

- 2003—Social media is born with the introduction of Myspace.

- 2004—Facebook is launched.

- 2007—Steve Jobs introduces the first iPhone.

3. Lyubomirsky, *How of Happiness,* 42.
4. MacLoad et al., *History of Just About Everything,*

Yet even living in what would be considered lavishness compared to our grandparents' days, we're not any happier. In fact, just the opposite holds true. Research published in the journal *Clinical Psychology Review* examined the differences in the rates of mental distress among high school and college students between 1938 and 2007. Their findings are remarkable. In 1938 roughly 5 percent of college students experienced clinical symptoms of mental illness, compared to 25 percent of college students in 2007. The authors of the report found that our rabid consumer culture seems to be a key factor in this equation, and write:

> As American culture has increasingly valued extrinsic and self-centered goals such as money and status, while increasingly devaluing community, affiliation, and finding meaning in life, the mental health of American youth has suffered . . . materialism, individualism, and impossibly high expectations have led to an epidemic of poor mental health in the U.S. and other Western nations.[5]

While the research telling us that materialism won't bring lasting happiness is well established, it is the underlying principle of why this is the case that is most interesting. As human beings the laws of nature bind us. We may not like that fact, but are subject to this reality nonetheless. Having money and buying things does feel good in the short term. It's fun to pull out cash or our credit card and feel the power of the purchase. When we get what we want we feel good, as dopamine is released in our brains and gives us the sensation of pleasure.

However, that high we experience soon wears off, and we're back to our normal state of being. This occurs because we are hardwired to naturally adjust from those peak times of both pleasure and pain back to homeostasis. Psychologists have coined this behavioral principle "hedonic adaptation." They also use the term "hedonic treadmill" to refer specifically to our attempts to experience lasting peace and joy from passing pleasure. They use this term to present the image of a hamster, running round and round

---

5. Twenge et al, "Birth Cohort Increases in Psychopathology," 146.

on a wheel, but going nowhere. In the same way we can buy the newest cell phone, happy meal, or Starbucks blend coffee, but it won't contribute to a lasting sense of peace and well-being.

Culturally, this idea that we would somehow become happier through consumption began to take hold in the United States after World War II. Prior to this time most people didn't have much discretionary income. All of the money they earned would go toward the basics of food, shelter, clothing, and transportation. However, with the advent of the war, our nation began to mass-produce a virtual entire economy of goods to support the war effort. In addition to the production, we developed a host of technologies in areas such as food preservation, vehicle and airplane manufacturing, and textile and communications development.

But what lit the spark of what is now our consumer culture were the business changes that took place during the 1950s. Historians Douglas T. Miller and Marion Nowak point to ways in which companies manipulated the general public, thereby creating *consumers*, whether those consumers could afford their products or not:

> To make certain that people could purchase the products that advertising convinced them they needed, credit was vastly extended in the fifties. Poverty, Henry Luce assured Americans in 1956, was merely the "habit of thinking poorly". There was no need to think poorly in the fifties. Even without the money you could have the goods. It was of course necessary to convince people that the old American habit of thrift was no longer a sacred virtue. Motivational researcher Dr. Ernest Dichter, in a bulletin to businessmen, described the problem of changing people's values from thrift to spending: "We are now confronted with the problem of permitting the average American to feel moral ... even when he is spending, even when he is not saving, even when he is taking two vacations a year and buying a second or third car. One of the basic problems of prosperity, then, is to demonstrate

that the hedonistic approach to his life is a moral, not an immoral one.[6]

We've come a long way since the 1950s, but this business principle hasn't changed. Corporations have continued to employ progressively stealthy psychological tactics to create new generations of consumers. And they have done so in subtle and creative ways, such as cradle to grave techniques targeting toddlers, with the goal of branding lifelong customers. Their wild success stands as evidence to the principle of hedonic adaptation. If buying and having brought genuine contentment, then the US should be the most relaxed and happiest nation in the entire world.

DOMINANCE OF THE
MEDICAL MODEL OF ILLNESS

Since the time of Cannon and Selye's finding on stress, there have been tremendous advancements in understanding contributors to physical and behavioral health. Critically important medical breakthroughs have occurred during the past century, including the discovery of penicillin, magnetic resonance imaging (MRI), angioplasty (a surgical procedure to widen narrowed or blocked arteries), statins (cholesterol lowering drugs), kidney dialysis, and endoscopic surgery, as well as kidney and liver transplants.

However, these wonderful technological advancements in health care have brought with it the perception that any and all ailments are now relics of the past. There exists a cultural perception that some product must be out there to "fix" our afflictions. As many legitimate products and procedures that have been developed there are now at least as many dubious ones on the market. The Internet alone is flooded with every conceivable promise of increased health. From loss of weight to increase in libido, mail-order products flood the market. Scholars have recognized the cultural shift and use the term "Scienciness"[7] that refers to attaching

6. Miller and Nowak, *Fifties,* 117.
7. Weitz, *Sociology of Health,* 13.

the aura of scientific research to non-proven goods in order to sell the public on the latest snake oil products.

One of the best examples of this is the weight-loss industry. These corporations have developed a net worth in the billions by selling products that for a majority of people simply don't work. Their financial success is due primarily to fooling consumers into thinking there is some magic bullet that will shed pounds without engaging in regular exercise and decreasing caloric intake. Not only are such products ineffective for long-term weight-loss for most folks, but many of these products use synthetic chemicals that can even cause harm. The US Food and Drug Administration (FDA), in monitoring these products, cautions:

> We've also found weight-loss products marketed as sup
> plements that contain dangerous concoctions of hidden
> ingredients including active ingredients contained in ap-
> proved seizure medications, blood pressure medications,
> and antidepressants.[8]

The allure for these products is understandable of course. It would be nice to have a magic pill for our problems. And with the advances medicine has made in a host of areas, such as cancer treatment and high cholesterol, it can be hard to know what works and what doesn't. Yet weight management comes down to nature. With the exception of those with unique medical conditions, for the rest of us our weight is determined by balance our caloric intake with physical activity. And as for weight loss, the FDA finds that "The only natural way to lose weight is to burn more calories than you take in."[9]

In modern times the very term "health" conjures up ideas primarily about our physical bodies. Am I sick or healthy? And if I am sick how can I get fixed? This dualistic view has been driven by the prominence of the *medical model* of health and illness, which has been dominant during the past century. The medical model basically refers to what doctors mean when they say a

---

8. US Food and Drug Administration, "Beware of Products," para. 5.

9. US Food and Drug Administration, "Beware of Products," para. 8.

person is ill. But that view limits the understanding of health to one dimension—biology.

During the past 40 years a more holistic model of health has emerged, which takes into account other elements of being human in addition to biology. These include emotions, relationships, psychological make-up, and spirituality. This model has been referred to as the sociological model,[10] as well as the more descriptive biopsychosocial-spiritual model of health and illness.

The biopsychosocial model can be traced to a classic article by George Engel titled *The Need for a New Medical Model: a Challenge for Biomedicine*,[11] published in the journal *Science* nearly thirty years ago in 1992, 66 years after the concept of stress was born in Selye's mind.

Engel was a professor of psychiatry and medicine at the University of Rochester's School of Medicine. He makes the case that all of medicine, not just psychiatry, is hindered by reliance on the biomedical model due to its one-dimensional view of human nature. This view "leaves no room within its framework for the social, psychological, and behavioral dimensions of illness."[12] Engle adds that the medical model is not only the leading model, but that it has become entrenched in our cultural understanding of what constituted "health" and "illness." He writes:

> The biomedical model has thus become a cultural imperative, its limitations easily over-looked. In brief, it has now acquired the status of *dogma*. In science, a model is revised or abandoned when it fails to account adequately for all the data. A dogma, on the other hand, requires that discrepant data be forced to fit the model or be excluded.[13]

Engel goes on to point out that while very useful, strict reliance upon the medical model limits effective care for patients, because it breaks with the holistic natures of human beings. At a minimum

10. Weitz, *Sociology of Health*, 103.
11. See Engel, "Need for a New Medical Model."
12. Engel, "Need for a New Medical Model," 319.
13. Engel, "Need for a New Medical Model," 319-20.

he points to the need for doctors to possess the soft skills of educating and emotionally supporting their patients as they face the challenges of living with a particular disease.[14]

In championing the biopsychosocial model of health, Engel makes the humble and critically important point that what we understand as "health" or "illness" is often subjective to the individual. The concept of well-being goes far beyond laboratory tests, physical limitations, and stage of life. He points to the not-uncommon experience for patients to test positive for some needed treatment, who feel fine, as well as those with a full medical work-up indicating health, but feel sick, as was my own case a few years back.[15] More to the point, the biopsychosocial model of health recognizes that cultural, social, psychological, environmental, and other relevant factors come together to make up a person's *well-being*.

This holistic model of health simply points to what is obvious to most people. Our well-being is made up of many factors. While different to each person's situation, we're all affected by social relationships, emotional ups and downs, our thoughts, our personalities, ourhabitual behaviors (some healthy, some not so), and our beliefs about the meaning of life. All of these are in addition to our biological make-up and come together to create our sense of wellness.

MEDICALIZATION

The final of the three forces contributing to higher levels of distress in society is "medicalization." Peter Conrad has studied this cultural phenomenon much over the past forty years and is a leading expert in his field. He cut his teeth on this topic with his dissertation work that examined the medicalization of overactive children. Conrad defines medicalization as "the process by which

---

14. Engel, "Need for a New Medical Model," 324.
15. Engel, "Need for a New Medical Model," 326.

nonmedical problems become defined and treated as medical problems, usually in terms of illness and disorders."[16]

This means that problems with living that are common to the human condition are increasingly being viewed through a medical lens. Examples of medicalization include baldness, childbirth, menopause, andropause (male menopause), pre-menstrual system (PMS), and deviant teenage behaviors. Even the natural process of aging is now largely considered an illness requiring treatment.

Historically, we can see this emergence of medicalization through changes in what is considered to be the "bible" of mental illness, the *Diagnostic and Statistical Manual of Mental Disorders*, known as the DSM, now in its fifth major revision. The DSM was first published in 1952 and contained criteria for 128 categories of mental illness. The manual's length was 132 pages. 61 years later, in 2013, the number of diagnoses had ballooned to 541, and listed in a book with a page count just shy of 1,000.[17]

The exponential increase in problems with living being categorized as medical conditions requiring formal treatment is troubling at two key levels. First, casting wider and wider nets into the sea of life's difficulties means more and more people will be caught up in being labeled. The medical industry is just that, an industry, and one of the largest in the country. Health care costs in the US is over 3 trillion dollars and accounts for roughly 20 percent of the gross domestic product. More patients being labeled as having a disease also mean more customers for health-related businesses.

The second concern is perhaps even more troubling. As we increasingly define problems with living as medical conditions, more of us are likely to experience self-labeling, where we define ourselves by what ails us. A diagnostic label often becomes a master status or our sense of *self* at our very core. A person understandably nervous when speaking to a group of people now takes on the label *social anxiety disorder*. Having thin eyelashes requires medical treatment for *hypotrichosis*. Drinking too much coffee leads to *caffeine intoxication*.

16. Conrad, *Medicalization of Society*, 4.
17. Blashfield et al., "Cycle of Classification," 32.

Medicalization occurs in both physical and behavioral health, but it is most evident in psychology and psychiatry. Of all the mental disorders, perhaps the best example of medicalization can be seen in the diagnoses of depression. Clinical depression is a genuine medical condition and is one of the most debilitating and painful experiences to live with. However, the symptoms that mark depression are also quite common. All of us are not likely but *guaranteed* to experience depressive symptoms during our lives. We will all lose people we love, become ill, experience setbacks, and be sad at times. Because there are not biological tests for any mental illness, clinicians must rely on a checklist of symptoms to determine whether a person has a medical illness or if the symptoms are simply part of the difficulties of life.

It is challenging to compare levels of depression today with those prior to the 1950s, since the DSM was not first developed and published until 1952. However, since the development of the DSM, rates of depression have been rising. There is no shortage of writings devoted to this cultural phenomenon.

Nearly 20 years ago, when I was completing my own dissertation on college students' mental health, I reviewed the academic literature related to several variables, one of them being depression. The consensus even then was that college-counseling centers, for the past 30 years, had transitioned from career advisement and skill development to mental health counseling, primarily because of the rise in behavioral health issues among students.

Depression has become so common that over the past several decades it is often called "the common cold of mental illness." This implies that most people will "get it" at some point in their lives.

Martin Seligman, a leading writer in the new field of positive psychology, uncovers a critically important contradiction when thinking about such clinical sadness in the midst of material abundance. He writes:

> Mounting over the last forty years in every wealthy country on the globe, there has been a startling increase in depression. Depression is now ten times as prevalent as it was in 1960, and it strikes at a much younger age. The

mean age of a person's first episode of depression forty years ago was 29.5, while today it is 14.5 year. This is a paradox, since every objective indicator of well-being—purchasing power, amount of education, availability of music, and nutrition—has been going north, while every indicator of subjective well-being has been going south. How is this epidemic to be explained?[18]

Seligman answers his own question first by taking on the easy part of this question—what are *not* the causes. He identifies three areas that can be ruled out: biology, ecology, and lack of resources.

Biology cannot play a role, since there's virtually no chance that we've experienced genetic changes in just the last half-century. From an ecological standpoint, the rise in depression makes no sense in the US, as our sanitation and food quality are among the highest standards in the world. Seligman points to an Amish community who live just outside of Philadelphia as an example. They live in the same general environment as those in the city of brotherly love, but experience exponentially lower rates of depression. And finally, depression cannot be traced to a lack of material goods, since high levels of depression occur only in affluent countries.

Seligman, through his research and study of depression, discovered that the rise in unhappiness in our culture could be attributed to, at least in part, what he termed *learned helplessness*. Learned helplessness is a state of mind marked by the belief that we are trapped in some negative state of life, *even when the condition is escapable.* To say that another way, we can learn (incorrectly) that the adverse situation we are experiencing is beyond any hope of relief (when relief is actually possible).

Depression serves as a case study to the problem of medicalization, in that it points to overemphasis of viewing behavioral through a strictly medical lens. It sends the message that when life's difficulties arise there *must* be some pill or product on the

18. Seligman, *Authentic Happiness,* 118-19.

market to alleviate our sufferings. After all, look at the technological progress we see all around, even compared to one generation ago.

The desire to escape all discomfort and suffering is natural, but not possible, since sorrow in life is to be expected from time to time. And while not pleasant, it's often healthy, as strange as that may sound. That's because the more we cling to the idea that distress in life is unnatural, the more pain and anguish we will feel when we go through tough times. This same principle holds true for our physical health. If we avoid exercise, over time our muscles will atrophy and we will grow weak. We also see this in nutrition and sanitation. If we avoid any exposure to germs in our environment, our immune system weakens instead of becoming stronger. Evidence for this can be seen in the book captivatingly titled *Eat Dirt,* by Dr. Josh Axe.

Axe presents an array of medical research that support what has become known as the "hygiene hypothesis." The hygiene hypothesis is the suggestion that too *little* exposure to common bacteria, especially as a child, often leads to a host of physical ailments. Such illnesses include diabetes, various food allergies, migraine headaches, irritable bowel syndrome, as well as anxiety and depression, to name just a few. The reason this happens is that, culturally, we've bought into the idea that our bodies should operate as a fortress under siege by microbial enemies that seek to lay waste to our good health. When, in fact, good health is the result of a very complex interaction of natural microorganisms working to keep our bodies in a balanced state of good (but never "perfect") health. Axe writes:

> For the past century, in so many facets of our lives, we've been trying to blast bacteria. The goal was understandable: bugs bad, clean good. But in our misguided attempt to keep ourselves and our families safe, we have exposed ourselves to a growing health crisis. We have oversanitized our daily lives, and our bodies, relying on disinfectants and sanitizers, spending most of our time indoors, and rushing to get prescriptions for antibodies any time we (or our kids) feel sick. Now we know that living in too

sterile of an environment makes our bodies more vulnerable to disease, not less . . . Now we know that what's most threatening is our modern lack of "old friends", the commensal and mutualist bacteria and other microbes in our microbiome that help fine-tune our immune responses to our environment.[19]

This revelation of the ironic link between overreliance on medicine leading to worse physical health outcomes applies likewise to behavioral health. The more we are medicalized to counter the natural problems that come along with life, the less able we'll be to handle life's difficulties. Axe summarizes this point when writing about "germs and dirt," but the same holds true if we substitute for those terms "stress and effort":

By living in a squeaky-clean bubble and turning germs and dirt [stress and effort] into villains to be destroyed or avoided at all costs, we've kept some of our most powerful allies for health at arm's length.[20]

19. Axe, *Eat Dirt,* 49.
20. Axe, *Eat Dirt,* 49.

3

Rethinking S.T.R.E.S.S.

THIS NEXT SECTION PROPOSES a new way of looking at how we might think about stress. This perspective is based on the holistic model of health to perhaps counter the dated notion that stress is one-dimensional, yet still in keeping with Selye's basic understanding of stress as "the non-specific response of the body to any demand for change," which is foundational to life.

This holistic model of health simply points to what is obvious to most people. Our well-being is comprised of many factors. While unique to each person's situation, we all share social relationships, emotional ups and downs, thinking patterns, personalities, habitual behaviors (some healthy, some not so) and beliefs about the meaning of life. All of these are in addition to our biological make-up and come together to form our sense self. This model highlights the importance of embracing these elements—the natural (Simplify), psychological (Think), emotional (Resilience), biological (Exercise), Spiritual, and Social components of life.

Each acronym is composed of three sections. The first is an *illustration* to offer a mental image. This is followed by *motivation* that provides rationale based on research in this area. Then lastly is an *application* of basic ways to implement these natural ways of de-stressing.

One day, when writing this part of the manual, I became aware of how basic this subject matter came across to me. That same day I read an article that serves as a marker to perhaps how far our culture has strayed from simple truths.

In September of 2018, the American Academy of Pediatrics published an article titled "The Power of Play: A Pediatric Role in Enhancing Development in Young Children." Here the authors make the case that as a society, we've forgotten about the role of play in a child's life and the importance of having positive relationships for healthy development. The report reads:

> Play is not frivolous: it enhances brain structure and function and promotes executive function (ie, the process of learning, rather than the content), which allow us to pursue goals and ignore distractions. When play and safe, nurturing relationships are missing in a child's life, toxic stress can disrupt the development of executive function and the learning of prosocial behavior . . . The mutual joy and shared communication (harmonious serve and return interactions) that parents and children can experience during play regulate the body's stress response.[1]

One would hope that we've not reached a point in our culture where we need to rely on scholars to tell us that it's critically important for healthy child development that kids spend a good deal of time playing, or that it's is a good idea for adults, as parents and caretakers, to have fun with the children we love. But we may be nearing that point, as the authors of this article suggest that pediatricians write a "prescription for play"[2] to parents of young children. What follows are very elemental ways, much like play, to reconsider the role of stress in our lives and to rethink how we engage with the dailiness of life.

---

1. Yogman et al., "Power of Play," 1.
2. Yogman et al., "Power of Play, 10.

4

Simplify

S   t   r   e   s   s
i
m
p
l
i
f
y

Life is really simple, but we insist on making it complicated.

CONFUCIUS (551 BC–479 BC)

ILLUSTRATION

The Businessman and the Fisherman

A BUSINESSMAN TOOK A short vacation to a small Greek coastal village. Unable to sleep, he walked the pier. A small boat with just one fisherman had docked and inside the boat were several large tuna.

"How long did it take you to catch them?" he asked.

"Only a little while," the Greek fisherman replied.

"Why don't you stay out longer and catch more fish?" he asked.

"I have enough to support my family and give a few to friends," the Greek fisherman said as he unloaded them into a basket.

"But . . . What do you do with the rest of your time?"

The fisherman looked up and smiled, "I sleep late, fish a little, play with my children, take a nap with my wife, and stroll into the village, where I sip wine and play guitar with my friends."

The businessman laughed, "Sir, I am an MBA and can help you. You should fish more, and with the proceeds buy a bigger boat. In no time you could have several boats with the increased haul. Eventually you would have a fleet of fishing boats. Then instead of selling your catch to the middleman, you could sell directly to the consumers. You could control the product, processing, and distribution. You would need to leave this small coastal village and move to the city to run your expanding empire."

The fisherman asked, "But, sir, how long will all this take?"

"15–20 years, 25 tops," said the businessman.

"But what then?" asked the fisherman.

The businessman laughed and said, "That's the best part; when the time is right, you would announce an IPO and sell your company stock to the public and become very rich. You would make millions".

"Millions? Then what?" asked the fisherman.

The businessman replied, "Then you could retire and move to a small coastal fishing village, where you could sleep late, fish a little, play with your kids, take a nap with your wife, and stroll to the village in the evenings, where you could sip wine and play guitar with your friends."[1]

---

1. "Lessons From a Greek Fisherman."

MOTIVATION

We all experience challenges and difficulties in our lives. But we often bring these troubles upon ourselves. It just seems to be part of our human nature. Our minds and bodies were created with balance and warning mechanisms built right in. Our bellies growl when hungry, and ache from overeating. Emotions and thoughts guide behavior. We experience natural consequences from the choices we make.

Our need for balance may be most clearly seen in our sleep cycles. We are hardwired with an embedded "stop" and "go" system. During the 24 hours of a day, people sleep on average seven to eight hours during the night. Some sleep more, others less. During our time asleep, our minds go through different cycles that serve to regenerate our energies for the next day. Sleep scientists have found that the most important time during sleep is also when we are most deeply slumbering. They have termed this cycle rapid eye movement, or REM sleep.

Yet many of us simply abuse these natural sleep patterns which are critical for good health. The Centers for Disease Control and Prevention (CDC) reports that roughly one-third of American adults don't get enough sleep, which is foundational to good physical and emotional health.[2] Chronic sleep deprivation has long been associated with poor health outcomes and includes high blood pressure, obesity, and various behavioral health difficulties.

Regarding the idea of simplicity, perhaps the most striking writing I've come across in complicating life was captured in a 2005 book titled *Last Child in the Woods* written by Richard Louv. Louv makes the case that we are experiencing a host of increased behavioral problems, which he coins "Nature Deficit Disorder" (NDD), because we have lost our connection with nature. He points to many cultural changes that are keeping people indoors. Among these include the perceived fear of crime, driven by the media ratings war, and the explosion of the gaming industry. Louv

2. Centers for Disease Control, "1 in 3 Adults Don't Get Enough Sleep," line 1.

is not suggesting that NDD is an actual diagnosable mental illness. However, the phrase does seem to speak not only the importance of simplicity, but also healthy pleasures that have been lost in our consumer culture.[3]

Since the time of Louv's writing, a great deal of research has been conducted in this area. There is little question that overconsumption of social media is clearly associated with higher levels of distress and depression. Studies have found that the more "friends" we have on Facebook, the more isolated from others we feel. This paradox is not difficult to understand.

A 2017 Harvard Business article titled "A New, More Rigorous Study Confirms, the More You Use Facebook, the Worse You Feel" helps us understand that unquestionably, humans are social beings and need relationships to thrive. However, while social platforms are structured to mimic genuine friendship, somehow they fall short. Not only don't such sites make for genuine connections, use of Facebook leads to being less happy. The authors sum up their findings:

> Overall, our results showed that, while real-world social networks were positively associated with overall well-being, the use of Facebook was negatively associated with overall well-being. These results were particularly strong for mental health; most measures of Facebook use in one year predicted a decrease in mental health in a later year. We found consistently that both liking others' content and clicking links significantly predicted a subsequent reduction in self-reported physical health, mental health, and life satisfaction.[4]

Spending too much time on social media is analogous to enjoying a beautiful sunset versus looking at the image of a sunset on our computer screens. It's nice, but not real or satisfying. There seems to be something about nature that deeply nourishes the soul.

---

3. Louv, "Do Our Kids Have Nature-Deficit Disorder," 24-30.
4. Shakya and Christakis, "A New, More Rigorous Study Confirms," para. 6.

APPLICATION

"I'm happiest when I'm out of breath."

In the spring of 2017, near the end of the semester, I was teaching an introductory course in Sociology. We were covering a chapter on health and discussing what seems to make people happy and healthy. My students were working in groups and brainstorming those things that seem to bring them long-term happiness rather than those things that merely give passing pleasure such as food, shopping, and social media.

We discussed their replies as a class and one student, who was on our cross-country team, said something that has stuck with me. He said, "I'm happiest when I'm out of breath." When asked about what he meant, he elaborated that he feels a sense of pure joy when he runs competitively, even amidst the discomfort and pain that come with pushing his body to the limit.

There seems to be a sense of clarity and joy that comes along with the simple things of life. This student's experience speaks to the most basic element of life that most of us take for granted—our breathing. Being aware of and practicing deep inhales and exhales is a simple but effective way to bring calm into our lives.

Listen to your mother!

Several years ago I joined a listserv (an online group of people who share similar interests) regarding emerging research in positive psychology. This most recent school within psychology is only 20 years old but has taken hold like wild fire in academia and popular culture. One of the attractions to this line of study is that it focuses on discovering why people flourish so that we can better understand what leads to happiness and well-being.

One of the discussions on this listserv had to do with a pocket of research looking at the benefits for children of having grandparents who live in close proximity to them. A few points and findings from research studies were shared, teasing out this question. Then one of our members chimed in with: "do we really need a cost/benefit analysis to understand the benefits of kids spending time with their grandparents?" His point was that while research is extremely valuable, there are certain things in life that are self-evident.

This same idea of obvious benefits can be applied to spending time with Mother Nature. Being outside and breathing in fresh air is good for body, mind, and spirit. Endless supplemental activities are available for all tastes and interest. Some of us enjoy sports, taking walks, going for a run, or just taking in beautiful scenery. It's simply a good idea to make getting outside part of our daily habits.

A good night KISS

In our media obsessed culture it makes sense to follow the time-honored acronym KISS . . . Keep it Simple and get some Sleep! Of all basic components of good health, one of the most important is sleep. Medical studies have long confirmed what most people know by personal experience. The average person needs roughly 6 to 8 hours of sound sleep per night. Some of us can get by with less while others need more, but no one can function with inadequate slumber.

Part of ensuring good sleep is detaching from social media. Detachment is not the same as abstinence. We can still use, but in moderation. Part of the key here is to examine your lifestyle and what we use on a daily or weekly basis. We all at times think we are busier than we really are. How much of what we need to do is spending time on social media, versus work or study? What are the things we *need*, and what are those we *want*? Are our "wants" making us anxious or distressed? If so, we might consider cutting back or even giving them up.

A related area to the concept of simplification is our diet. Culturally we have made a habit of eating out, in no small part due to the hectic schedules that drive us. In 1970 Americans ate out on average 25 percent of the time. By 2015 we've reached a tipping point where we now eat out more than we prepare our own food.[5] The challenge with eating out so much is that statistically, prepared food is higher in calories and lower in nutrients. There is nothing wrong with splurging now and again, but eating basic, whole foods that are naturally designed to nourish (fruits, fish, grains, etc.) goes a long way in good health maintenance.

5. Cohen, "Americans Spend More Eating Out Than at Home."

5

Think

sTress
h
i
n
k

The mind is its own place and in itself can make a heaven of hell, a hell of heaven

JOHN MILTON (1606–1674)

ILLUSTRATION

The Two Wolves

AN OLD CHEROKEE CHIEF was teaching his grandson about life . . .
"A fight is going on inside me," he said to the boy. "It is a terrible fight and it is between two wolves.

"One is evil—he is anger, envy, sorrow, regret, greed, arrogance, self-pity, guilt, resentment, inferiority, lies, false pride, superiority, self-doubt, and ego.

"The other is good—he is joy, peace, love, hope, serenity, humility, kindness, benevolence, empathy, generosity, truth, compassion, and faith.

"This same fight is going on inside you—and inside every other person, too."

The grandson thought about it for a minute and then asked his grandfather,

"Which wolf will win?"

The old chief simply replied,

"The one you feed."[1]

MOTIVATION

The ability to think and reason is what separates us from animals. Our minds have incredible abilities. We can ponder, speak, write, create, converse, and pray. Our minds, to a large degree, give us control of our lives and destinies.

Within the social sciences, the discipline of psychology concerns itself most with understanding how the mind works. This major typically ranks as one of the top ten most popular programs, and is also one of the youngest academic fields, being less than 150 years old. Most introductory texts trace the founding of psychology to the year 1879 when Wilhelm Wundt founded the first research laboratory in Leipzig, Germany. Psychology grew out of the field of philosophy, which is primarily concerned with understanding how to live the good life, drawing upon great thinkers dating back to the sixth century BC.

Since its birth, most of psychology has been concerned with identifying and alleviating mental distress. While there are a great number of theorists who've tried to unpack the human psyche, their work can be classified within five major schools:

1. "The Two Wolves."

- Psychoanalysis—Places emphasis on the unconscious and conscious mind as well as the role of early childhood experiences.

- Behaviorism—Grew in large part as a reaction against psychoanalysis, and views behavior as a response to stimuli in a person's environment.

- Humanistic—Also known as the "third force" after psychoanalysis and behaviorism, views humans as inherently good but often distressed by the influence of negative but influential people in their lives.

- Cognition—Focuses on how the mind processes information through capacities such as thinking, memory, creating, and problem-solving.

- Positive Psychology—As its name implies, studies those *positive* traits that lead to a life of well-being and happiness.

Of all these, perhaps the one that's most relevant in helping people address distressing events is the cognitive school. Cognition refers to how the mind operates through its faculties such as thinking, reasoning, attention-reasoning, problem-solving, and memory. This school grew up alongside the development of mainframe and personal computer and uses similar terminology such as *processing information.*

A leading model of therapy that is used for a host of behavioral issues is known as *Cognitive Behavioral Therapy* (CBT). The power behind CBT is that it tells us that there is a strong connection between our emotions, decisions, and consequences in our lives. To say that another way, how we *perceive* a situation will impact our emotions (how we feel), and therefore what decisions we make and resulting outcomes. While a widely used form of therapy, the principles are very understandable. Our perspective about life drives our actions. How we *see* a situation directly affects our experience of it.

I see this every day on campus with my students. Those who see college as a very real opportunity to help them reach their professional goals come to class prepared and ready to learn and, most importantly, earn that A! Those who lack such a vision but are there mostly for the social events are less prepared when they come to class. They not only perform at a lower level academically but also enjoy their college years less, or at least it seems that way to me.

When teaching an introductory course in sociology, we look at the power of perspective through the lens of a 240-year-old true story about contrasting views on education. In 1774, Virginia officials proposed to teach Iroquois boys at the college of William and Mary, where they would be treated and taught just like the young colonialists. The Iroquois elders took some time to mull over the offer, then responded in the following spirited manner:

> *We know that you highly esteem the kind of learning taught in colleges, and that the maintenance of your young men, while with you, would be very expensive to you. We're convinced, therefore, that you mean to do us good by your proposal, and we thank you heartily. But you, who are wise, must know that different nations have different conceptions of things; and you will not, therefore, take it amiss if our ideas of this kind of education happens not to be the same with yours.*
>
> *We have had some experience of it. Several of our young people were formerly brought up in the colleges or the northern province. They were instructed in all your sciences. But when they came back to us, they were bad runners, ignorant of every means of living in the woods, unable to bear either cold or hunger, knew neither how to build a cabin, take a deer, or kill an enemy, spoke our language imperfectly, and therefore were neither fit for hunters, warriors, nor councilors. They were totally good for nothing.*
>
> *We are, however, not the less obliged for your kind offer, though we decline accepting. To show our grateful sense of it, if the gentlemen of Virginia shall send them a dozen of their sons, we would take great care in their education, instruct them in all we know, and make men of them.*[2]

2. Carroll, *Letters of a Nation*, 240.

This story shines light on competing notions of education, and also serves as a powerful metaphor for the power of perspective. How we perceive, meaning *see*, the circumstance of life goes a very long way in determining whether we flourish or flounder.

APPLICATION

You can't hit what you can't see.

During my time in the military I had a training experience that has always stayed with me because it applies to so many areas of life. We had advanced beyond basic marksmanship and were learning about tactics and how to engage the enemy. Our instructor told us that we should be confident in our shooting skills because we had qualified with our weapons on the rifle range. However, he cautioned us about not being overconfident, since there is a lot more to fighting than shooting well. Tactics and strategy are key in defeating the enemy. To make this point our instructor simply stated: "you can't hit a target if you can't see the target."

This lesson can apply to the subtle enemies we often face when caught up in the proverbial rat race of life. We go through the motions in most of our days responding to this and that demand of work, school, family, and friends. A powerful way to counter the feelings of being overwhelmed is to first *see* what causes us fear and distress. What are those daily habits we've fallen into that don't serve us well? Do we worry over how many "likes" we get on Facebook or hits we get on social media? Do we eat while watching TV every night, neither fully enjoying our meal or the show?

Selye used the term "eustress" for the positive stressors, and "distress" for the negative events that can drain us. But we've learned that both types of stress make demands upon our energy and sap our recourses. Even doing things that are *fun* can turn negative when they take us away from our responsibilities. Like the wolf fable teaches us, what we feed becomes dominant in our lives. Being proactive and identifying what causes us distress enables us to face and defeat the hidden wolves in our lives.

The power of now.

In a book about stress, it may seem overly simplistic to champion the idea of living in the moment. Especially when we live in a culture that is screaming at us to continually buy, do, or eat something. Added to this is the avalanche of news media vying to sway us left or right, and the distractions abound.

Yet when it comes right down to it we can only live in the moments of time. As each second passes, it is gone forever. And our futures are in no way guaranteed, and a glance on any obituary section of a newspaper will confirm that.

Hopefully this is an empowering notion, since it means that we can largely control our actions and savor those especially good moments. As for the difficult times, we are also comforted with the knowledge that those moments, like all moments, will pass.

Look for the monster under your bed.

One of the surest ways to overcome our fears is to face them. Part of our human condition is that we all must face the ultimate reality and a fear most of us naturally share—our mortality. Ultimately, we must come to terms with the fact that we will die. Our understanding of the meaning of our physical death drives a great deal of how we live.

This same principle holds true to the smaller fears we face, even going back to our childhood. All children share that feeling or dream that there is something that comes in the night meaning to harm them. The scary, mythical creature usually hides in the closet or under the bed at night and can create a sense of terror that is palatable. Perhaps nothing is worse than that helpless feeling. Yet only when the child works up the courage to look under the bed to see nothing more than dust and some dirty clothes does she or he realize that there was nothing to be afraid of after all.

6

Resilience

```
s   t   R   e   s   s
        e
        s
        i
        l
        i
        e
        n
        c
        e
```

If all you can do is crawl, start crawling.

RUMI (1207–1273)

ILLUSTRATION

Good and Bad Luck

HERE IS A CHINESE story of a farmer who used an old horse to till his fields. One day, the horse escaped into the hills and when the farmer's neighbors sympathized with the old man over his bad luck, the farmer replied, "Bad luck? Good luck? Who knows?" A week later, the horse returned with a herd of horses from the hills and this time the neighbors congratulated the farmer on his good luck. His reply was, "Good luck? Bad luck? Who knows?"

Then, when the farmer's son was attempting to tame one of the wild horses, he fell off its back and broke his leg. Everyone thought this very bad luck. Not the farmer, whose only reaction was, "Bad luck? Good luck? Who knows?"

Some weeks later, the army marched into the village and conscripted every able-bodied youth they found there. When they saw the farmer's son with his broken leg, they let him off. Now was that good luck or bad luck?

Who knows?

Everything that seems on the surface to be an evil may be a good in disguise. And everything that seems good on the surface may really be an evil. So we must bear all the circumstances that life brings with equanimity and resilience and with an attitude that this too shall pass.[1]

MOTIVATION

Perhaps one of the most intriguing areas that has emerged in health studies during the past 20 years is in the area of *resilience*. Resilience refers to the capacity to bounce back from difficult life experiences that are part of every life, such as failures, sickness, and disappointments. This is an especially important part of the holistic model of health because it is a trait that directly counters our cultural notion that *stress* is an abnormal part of life.

Living with various types of strain is *natural* to every person who has ever lived. It is literally impossible to go through life without unpleasant experiences. Every human being shares trials and suffering. At some point we all become ill, even if it's nothing more than a cold or flu. Not all of our relationships are perfect,

---

1. "Good Luck? Bad Luck? Who Knows?" 1.

meaning people will let us down. We will all make mistakes and let ourselves down. Our loved ones, at some point in time, will die. And even if we are fortunate to live a full life that averages 80 years, we will one day die.

Much of our lives are, in essence, a battle. This has been recognized throughout all of history. Plato himself said to "be kind, for everyone you meet is fighting a hard battle." Resilience is the habit of mind that recognizes that life will, at times, be difficult, but that good can come from suffering. Sometimes the good is seen in obvious ways, sometimes not.

Our society has gone adrift from fostering the notion of resilience. The ironic reason for this is that along with the benefits of technological advancements has come the misconception that suffering is unnatural to how life should unfold.

My students and I discuss this in our "Sociology of Health and Illness" class. While we've made wonderful leaps medically, along with those advances come the belief that any undesirable but normal part of being human can be fixed, usually with some medical product. As mentioned earlier, Peter Conrad was one of the first to uncover this cultural phenomenon is his book *The Medicalization of Society.* Conrad details how, as a culture, we've become dazzled by the very legitimate wonders medicine offers, from life-saving drugs to remarkable surgical procedures. But along with these blessings has come a disconnect with reality. He writes: "One of the ironies of our culture is that no matter how much health is improved (as evidenced by decreased mortality rates, increased life expectancy, and improved health care), the reporting of health problems continues to rise."[2]

Christopher Lane, professor at Northwestern and author of *Shyness: How Normal Behavior Became a Sickness,* in one of his talks on medicalization made the observation that:

> Medicalization isn't the most elegant noun . . . but it's the best one we have for describing how common emotions and traits are turned into treatable conditions. Bad breath becomes halitosis, for example, and impotence

2. Conrad, *Medicalization of Society,* 149.

erectile dysfunction. Even overdoing plastic surgery gets a brand-new name: body dysmorphic disorder. To put it bluntly, this process of pathologizing has gotten out of control. It's become a juggernaut that no one seems able to stop.[3]

At a basic level it's rather simple to comprehend why medicalization has taken root and flourished. Culturally we've abandoned the notion that pain and struggle are normal and even a part of a healthy life. No one *wants* to suffer. However, when we deny elemental truths about life we set ourselves up for failure. We let our defenses down. We experience atrophy and grow weak.

APPLICATION

Run in the rain

Key to building resilience is to first recognize the need for it. Everyone faces challenges that must be overcome during the course of their lives. Yet our consumer culture has seeped into our collective conscious, giving us the message that some-*thing* will solve our problems. But as the maxim goes, life is a journey, not a destination. We never really reach full release from our cares here on earth.

With this in mind it's a good idea to do something, habitually, which takes us out of our comfort zone. Of course, we want to be sensible in our choices here, and not select activities that are likely to cause us harm. One of my favorite ways to do this has long been to go for a run in the rain. When I began to take runs as a teenager I remember thinking "It's raining outside . . . can't run today."

Then, over time as I did run in the rain, I had a liberating sensation. When I started, I could feel that it was raining, but as I got into the run my sense of things changed. It was as if I became part of the rain. No longer did the showers seem foreign, but natural. Stretching our capacities in spirit, body, and mind helps to make

---

3. "On the Medicalization of Our Culture", para. 4.

us stronger, and therefore more able to deal with difficulties as they arise.

Live like (weight) lifters!

Perhaps the easiest way to understand the principle of resilience is to consider how weight lifters grow stronger. When lifting heavy weights, what occurs in our physiology is actually a breakdown of muscle fibers. Our micro fibers and cells are torn and destroyed. But with nutrition and rest our muscles not only repair themselves, but actually grow bigger and stronger than they were before the "damage" that occurred by repetitive lifting.

We can use this example from sports as a metaphor for the challenging times in our lives. When we experience setback and strains we can call upon our resources to not only survive trials, but even to thrive as a result of the supposed damage that was inflicted. This very concept has been seen in studies of soldiers who return from battles who instead of experiencing post-traumatic stress disorder (PTSD) instead experience post-traumatic growth (PTG).

Find your role model.

The study of resilience is fascinating in part because it speaks to something that resonates in all of us. This term is from the Latin *resiliens* meaning to come "back," to "rebound". It is universally appealing because we all experience this in our own lives. Some experience very common recoveries from a cold, flu, or sprained ankle. Others face more profound setbacks such as loss of work, poor health, or broken relationship.

Because resilience is archetypical to the human experience, even our culture is captivated by its importance in the human experience. Perhaps the most common theme in Hollywood is that of resilience. Classic Disney films from *Snow White and the Seven*

Dwarfs to *The Jungle Book,* from *The Lion King* to *Moana,* are all stories showcasing this trait.

The same holds true for real life as well. There are any number of lives we can look to and study as examples and role models for us to learn from. St. Teresa of Avila, Abraham Lincoln, and Martin Luther King Jr. are classic illustrations, but most of us also know of less famous but equally powerful examples of resilience. Such admirable souls come from all walks of life and help us gain perspectives of hope and even humor in the midst of adversity.

7

Exercise

s   t   r   E   s   s
              x
              e
              r
              c
              i
              s
              e

If you are in a bad mood go for a walk.
If you are still in a bad mood go for another walk.

HIPPOCRATES (460 BC–370 BC)

ILLUSTRATION

Health and Humor

TWO MEN WERE HIKING one day out in the forest. They came across a bear.

One man took off his pack, pulled out a pair of running shoes, and started to put them on.

The friend frantically said, "You can't outrun that bear."

The other man calmly replied, "I don't need to. I only need to outrun you."[1]

MOTIVATION

Exercise is a solid foundation to good health in general, and when dealing with stress in particular. When thinking about exercise it is perhaps natural to think that the topic is limited to the physical element of our being. But the body cannot be separated from the mind and spirit any more than four seasons are isolated from a year, or each of the 24 hours from a day. Each element plays a particular role yet remains part of the whole.

Exercise is key to wellness since our beings are "housed" within our bodies. In scholarly writing on managing stress, regular exercise is virtually always at or near the top of every list. There are three main reasons for this.

First, we are physical beings. We also have a mind and spirit, but we are biological creatures. We experience life through our five senses—sight, hearing, taste, smell, and touch.

Next, from a neurobiological perspective, we are created for movement. When we engage in physical exertion our brains release neurotransmitters, which are chemicals that send signals and sensations throughout our nervous system. Medical researchers have identified a host of neurotransmitters (and are finding more everyday) but the two most commonly associated with exercise are dopamine and norepinephrine. When these chemicals are released we experience a heightened sense of strength, well-being, and calmness. We feel happier. That is why we use the phrase "runner's high" to describe the sense of euphoria runners feel during and at the completion of their training. This "high" is experienced by any strenuous activity, since the pleasurable sensation is not the result

1. "10 Short Parables on Love and Relationship," para. 3.

of any particular workout but from the release of chemicals in the brain.

Finally, regular physical training also ranks at the top of stress release studies because it is so customizable. One doesn't need to be a runner or any other particular athlete to get the tremendous benefits of exercise. As long as the workout is selected wisely by age, aptitude, and health risk assessments, exercise can be a healthy and enjoyable lifetime pursuit. In our sports-crazed culture it comes as no surprise that people now enjoy an endless variety of exercise.

While research has long supported the benefits of regular exercise, more recent studies tease out nuanced findings that are surprising. One is the misconception that we need to have a grueling workout to get any benefits from exercise. This seems to not be the case.

Researchers Ashna Samani and Matthew Heath from the School of Kinesiology at the University of Western Ontario examined the impact that just ten minutes of exercise has on mental focus.[2] In their study young adults were recruited and divided into two groups. The first would sit and spend ten minutes just reading a magazine. The other would work out on an exercise bike for the same amount of time. Once both had completed the activity they were hooked up to electronic devices that analyzed their reaction times while they completed an eye movement test. This test assessed student's ability to perform executive function tasks, such as organization, planning, and processing information.

The findings showed that the exercise group fared much better than those who sat and read. When discussing their findings Heath noted that "Those who had exercised showed immediate improvement. Their responses were more accurate and their reaction times were up to 50 milliseconds shorter than their pre-exercise values. That may seem minuscule but it represented a 14-percent gain in cognitive performance in some instances."[3]

2. Samani and Heath, "Executive-related oculomotor control is improved," 73-81.

3. University of Western Ontario, "Short-term exercise equals big-time brain boost," para. 4.

Heath adds "I always tell my students before they write a test of an exam or go into an interview—or do anything that is cognitively demanding—they should get some exercise first."[4]

These findings show that even small bursts of exercise can be helpful to our daily functioning. It also helps to dismiss the notion that we need to spend hours in a gym to reap the benefits that workouts offer. There is no shortage of research on the value of this foundational component of well-being and stress relief.

APPLICATION

Sweat the small stuff.

During the past century the nutrition and exercise industry has exploded. While our geographic residence may limit access to a local gym or health club, there is no shortage of exercise equipment or nutritional supplement available online or in stores. That is in additional to the virtually endless combination of body weight activities that can provide a top quality workout at literally no cost in terms of equipment needed.

Having access to exercise equipment is a good thing, but there is no magic that occurs just by belonging to a health club. In fact, such clubs have only existed for the past 70 years since 1936, when Jack LaLanne opened the first gym in Oakland, California.[5] Prior to this time folks were still able to lead healthy lives largely through good nutrition and exercise. However, exercise then was engaging in manual labor for many as well as spending less time indoors and in front of screens.

Fortunately, it is now common to hear about the importance of regular excise in society. This has risen, in large part, to counter the obesity epidemic of the past few decades. However *regular exercise* doesn't necessarily equate with paying for a gym membership and limiting our workout to those small pockets of time we

4. University of Western Ontario, "Short-term exercise equals big-time brain boost", para. 6.

5. Goldman, "Jack LaLanne Leads Others to Fitness," para. 3.

spend in such buildings. Walking up a flight of stairs instead of taking the elevator, spending time outside running around with nieces and nephews can all be part of an effective, natural, and affordable exercise routine.

The drug of choice

One of the most well established findings in health studies is that regular exercise is beneficial to our well-being. Physical training can take the form of cardiovascular activities, weights, stretching, and any number of tailored programs. Strength and conditioning regiments help to strengthen our heart, lungs, and muscles.

However, an additional benefit of exercise is that it releases hormones that are good for our mental health. When we work out, dopamine is released in our brain. Dopamine is a chemical that gives us a sense of pleasure and comfort. This is the same pleasure chemical that is released when we eat a piece of chocolate or receive a text message.

In fact, the benefits of exercise are so profound that some researchers have suggested that we now consider *prescribing* exercise, much like a prescription drug. Instead of seeing exercise as uncomfortable choices we need to do, we can envision it as a treat because of its plentiful benefits. The key is finding the activities, just like foods, that we naturally enjoy.

Double the fun

Whether or not we look forward to making a habit of regular exercise, one simple way to take it up a notch is to make it a social event. Taking a walk, weight lifting, or virtually any other activity tends to be more fun with other people.

Research reported in the Journal of the American Osteopathic Association examined the effects of group exercise on medical students. Medical school can be an especially demanding time for students due to the financial, academic, and personal demands placed upon these future physicians. In addition, students often lead sedentary lives due to the grueling demands of such training.

The design of the study was to place students into one of three groupings. One group who took part in a group fitness class, another group who exercised on their own, and a final group who did not take part in any physical training during the three-month study. The authors found that those who took part in group exercise experience both lower stress levels and scored higher on perceived levels of well-being than either those who exercised alone and those who did not work out regularly.[6]

At no other time in history has the average person enjoyed more access to group exercise. Gym memberships, fun runs, yoga, dance, biking, and even fitness boot camps are just some of the programs available to match our interests, build health, and reduce stress.

6. Yorks et al., "Effects of Group Fitness Classes on Stress and Quality of Life," 17-25.

8

Social

s   t   r   e   S   s
          o
          c
          i
          a
          l

There is nothing more on this earth more to be prized than
true friendship

ST. THOMAS AQUINAS (1225–1274)

ILLUSTRATION

Merry Christmas

DURING WORLD WAR I, on and around Christmas Day 1914, the
sounds of rifles firing and shells exploding faded in a number of

places along the Western Front in favor of holiday celebrations in the trenches and gestures of goodwill between enemies.

Starting on Christmas Eve, many German and British troops sang Christmas carols to each other across the lines, and at certain points the Allied soldiers even heard brass bands joining the Germans in their joyous singing.

At the first light of dawn on Christmas Day, some German soldiers emerged from their trenches and approached the Allied lines across the no man's land, calling out "Merry Christmas" in their enemies' native tongues. At first, the Allied soldiers feared it was a trick, but seeing the Germans unarmed they climbed out of their trenches and shook hands with the enemy soldiers. The men exchanged presents of cigarettes and plum puddings and sang carols and songs. There was even a documented case of soldiers from opposing sides playing a good-natured game of soccer.

Some soldiers used this short-lived ceasefire for a more somber task: the retrieval of the bodies of fellow combatants who had fallen within the no man's land between the lines.

The so-called Christmas Truce of 1914 came only five months after the outbreak of war in Europe and was one of the last examples of the outdated notion of chivalry between enemies in warfare. It was never repeated—future attempts at holiday ceasefires were quashed by officers' threats of disciplinary action—but it served as heartening proof, however brief, that beneath the brutal clash of weapons, the soldiers' essential humanity endured.

MOTIVATION

The social dimension of our lives is critical to our health and enjoyment of life. Our sense of connection comes from relationships with others. Such relationships often take the form of friends, classmates, neighbors, teammates, and coworkers.

In the course syllabi for all of my classes I detail the etymology, or origin, of the word "social" for my students. Social comes from the Latin *socius* which literally means "companion" or "ally."

The word "companion" can be traced to its original and means, "to break bread with."

One of the ways to see the importance of something is to look at what happens when that "thing" is no longer there. We can readily see this in social and physical structures. An organization without effective leadership soon becomes chaotic. A sports team without a captain has no leadership. If we take away food, we become malnourished, and after a few days without water we would die.

In the discipline of sociology one of the most critically important areas related to well-being is the process of socialization. Children who grow up in abusive or neglected homes are much more likely to experience behavioral challenges as adults than youth who grow up in functional, loving homes.

Positive social relationships are essential to our health. We, as humans, *are* social beings. We were not designed to live in isolation. Social science research has long established that people who have engaging, healthy relationships are happier and better able to cope with the normal stressors of everyday life.

Research reported in the *Journal of Health and Social Behavior* find that "individuals with the lowest level of involvement in social relationships are more likely to die than those with greater involvement" and that "the risk of death among men and women with the fewest social ties was more than twice as high as the risk for adults with the most social ties."[1]

And while the length of life on earth is important, so of course is its quality. Socially engaged people are also happier people. It is through developing and nourishing our relationships that we can share in the joys of life. Joy and fun are not traits belonging only to children. These experiences are essential to our well-being and serve as powerful defenses against the strain that at times comes with life. G.K. Chesterton, known as "the apostle of common sense," noted that:

---

1. Umberson and Karas, "Social Relationships and Health," para. 3.

It is not only possible to say a great deal in praise of play; it is really possible to say the highest things in praise of it. It might reasonably be maintained that the true object of all human life is play. Earth is a task garden; heaven is a playground. To be at last in such secure innocence that one can juggle with the universe and the stars, to be so good that one can treat everything as a joke—that may be, perhaps, the real end and final holiday of human souls.[2]

There is something about *play* that transcends age. And we can see evidence of this all around us. Prior to the Industrial Revolution most people had to work strenuous and often dangerous jobs every day for survival. But times and our economy have changed dramatically, especially since World War II, with sports emerging as a new force in our society. Recently some sociologists have included "sports" as the sixth major agent of socialization, in addition to family, school, peers, religion, and the media.

Relationships, engagement, and fun are all connected. They bring meaning and joy to life. I've tried to teach this to my own children, to help them to reframe in their mind the challenges they will face in life. For example, in their academic work it can be helpful to see the grade they want to earn as a challenge, just like scoring points in gymnastics, in a basketball game, or how many tackles they can make on a football field.

APPLICATION

You've got to write a letter to get a letter.

We human beings are social and physical by our nature. We were made for relationships. It's the smiles, handshakes, and hugs we share with others that release neurotransmitters, giving us that wonderful sense of euphoria and joy. This self-evident truth is also one of the most agreed-on research findings central to good health.

---

2. Chesterton, *All Things Considered*, 96.

Having a strong support group of family and friends is good for us in both good times and bad.

But good relationships don't happen all on their own. It's important to maintain old friends and also to make new ones. Part of that responsibility falls to us to reach out to and connect with others. There are many ways to engage in meaningful ways. One of the most important ones is to not take our current relationships with family and friends for granted, but to nurture them with regular contact.

It also makes sense to step out of our comfort zone and make new acquaintances. This can be done through volunteering, joining in faith activities, or even more fully engaging in our school or work.

Book some face-time with your friends.

When writing about the concept of stress in our current culture, it is obviously necessary to consider the impact of social media. This form of technology's impact on health is very interesting to think about, since there are clearly many benefits to being online. We can stay connected with others and find information instantaneously.

However, it is just as obvious that spending too much time online can be very harmful to our well-being. The allure of screen time can be captivating in a literal sense. We risk losing out on real, life-giving genuine experiences by settling for cheap, one-dimensional images on our displays.

Of all the modern ways in which distress has increased in society, too much screen time easily ranks as one of that can be most readily countered. For 99 percent of history, humans have had to struggle with the anxiety of finding enough food and shelter to survive. It's only in the last few decades that many of us are experiencing nervousness and anxiety over something we don't literally *need*. The good news is that along with this device comes the antidote to the worry it generates—an off button.

Take your medicine.

In medicine, *allopathic* care refers to treating illness by *opposites*. When we have a headache, we may take a pain reliever to counter the symptoms of a throbbing brain. When considering the daily grind of life, one of the best ways to counter a heavy spirit is with levity. As the old adage goes, "Angels can fly because they can take themselves too lightly."

We can infuse our days with the habit of play, joy, and laughter in many ways. In a general sense, we can choose and practice to be happy and to laugh readily. We've all likely met more than one person who seems to naturally have this quality. Several come to my mind, but one that stands out is Father Dan Reilly, a Franciscan friar and founder of Mount Irenaeus, a Franciscan retreat community. He is an extremely intelligent person who radiates a child-like joy to everyone he meets.

A great feature of play and laughter is that it's so easy to personalize. We can find it in our natural interests. Sports, being outdoors, playing games, or watching a good movie. When we smile and laugh endorphins are released. Endorphins are simply the body's *feel good* chemicals. These directly counter anxious feelings and give us a sense of euphoria and well being.

9

Spiritual

```
s  t  r  e  s  S
               p
               i
               r
               i
               t
               u
               a
               l
```

Let nothing disturb you. Let nothing frighten you.

St. Teresa of Avila (1515–1582)

ILLUSTRATION

Life and Death and Life

IN A MOTHER'S WOMB were two babies. The first baby asked the other: "Do you believe in life after delivery?"

The second baby replied, "Why, of course. There has to be something after delivery. Maybe we are here to prepare ourselves for what we will be later."

"Nonsense," said the first. "There is no life after delivery. What would that life be?"

"I don't know, but there will be more light than here. Maybe we will walk with our legs and eat from our mouths."

The doubting baby laughed. "This is absurd! Walking is impossible. And eat with our mouths? Ridiculous. The umbilical cord supplies nutrition. Life after delivery is to be excluded. The umbilical cord is too short."

The second baby held his ground. "I think there is something and maybe it's different than it is here."

The first baby replied, "No one has ever come back from there. Delivery is the end of life, and in the after-delivery it is nothing but darkness and anxiety and it takes us nowhere."

"Well, I don't know," said the twin, "but certainly we will see mother and she will take care of us."

"Mother?" The first baby guffawed. "You believe in mother? Where is she now?"

The second baby calmly and patiently tried to explain. "She is all around us. It is in her that we live. Without her there would not be this world."

"Ha. I don't see her, so it's only logical that she doesn't exist."

To which the other replied, "Sometimes when you're in silence you can hear her, you can perceive her. I believe there is a reality after delivery and we are here to prepare ourselves for that reality when it comes . . ."[1]

---

1. "In the Womb."

MOTIVATION

Of all the components of well-being, spirituality may be the one that has most changed during the past few decades, at least from a cultural perspective. There has been dramatic rise in the attraction of being "spiritual but not religious." At the same time there are signs that our society is becoming more open to again listening to what religion has to offer, perhaps because of the growing sense of cultural despair that permeates our society.

One example of this is a talk given by Bishop Robert Barron at the secular Google Headquarters in 2018 titled "Religion and the Opening up of the Mind." Barron anchors his talk on the relationship between the *search engine* developed by Google and the search engine that is hardwired into every human's heart—our search for God. Just as surfing the Internet often takes us far from our original search entry, so we can be taken far off-course when we worship things that don't quench our thirst, such as money, fame, power, and pleasure. Barron makes the point that because such passions don't truly satisfy, we can easily become overly attached if not addicted to them, losing our sense of peace and happiness.[2]

In the courses I teach on health one of the most powerful examples regarding spirituality and distress comes from our class on addiction. For many addicts, a powerful resource in overcoming addiction is the support group Alcoholics Anonymous (AA), founded in 1935. One particularly interesting aspect that highlights the profound impact spirituality can make has to do with the history of AA and the famous psychiatrist, Carl Jung.

Bill Wilson and Dr. Bob Smith founded AA. During a business trip to Ohio Bill, an alcoholic who had survived four hospital detox treatments was craving a drink. In an effort to not give into the temptation he made a phone call to a local minister, who through a series of calls put him in touch with a Dr. Bob, a surgeon and also an alcoholic. The men talked for hours and largely through the support of Dr. Bob, Bill never had another drink.

2. Barron, "Religion and the Opening up of the Mind."

What's interesting is that Dr. Bob never tried to *talk* Bill into sobriety but was simply there to offer his support.[3]

AA grew very quickly, largely due to its effectiveness in helping many people abstain from using alcohol. In a famous letter written by Carl Jung to Bill W., Jung offers an important insight to why spirituality is effective for so many alcoholics;

> You see, alcohol in Latin is *spiritus* and you use the same word for the highest religious experience as well as the most depraving poison. The helpful formula therefore is: *spiritus contra spiritum.*[4]

Here Jung is giving a literal plan of battling alcoholism with spirituality. While this story illustrates the role of faith by those who struggle with addiction, it can be applied to times of worry and difficulty in our daily lives.

Religion and spirituality have played a central role throughout the history of mankind, for both believers and non-believers. Vast volumes of works on this subject fill libraries throughout the world. They often champion different religious views and doctrines, but all of them share one elemental truth. We are mortal. We all will die. Those fortunate to live a full life will see only an average of 80 years on this earth. When compared to the earliest human civilization, which occurred roughly 10,000 years ago, that means we live during 0.008 % of all human history. That number is akin to the proverbial drop in the ocean.

Throughout all of human history, religious and spiritual practices have been a natural part of life. This holds true not only for individuals, but also for the community. Religious beliefs have been influential in providing care and support for the ill dating back to ancient times. Around 400 BC the first hospitals were built and dedicated to Asclepius, the Greek god of healing. These temple-hospitals were known as *asclepeions* and offered primitive forms of health care.

---

3. See Wilson, *Alcoholics Anonymous,* 94–95.
4. "Dr. Carl Jung's Letter to Bill W."

The Roman Catholic Church, since its founding, has had care of the poor and afflicted as part of its ethos. In fact, the Church is the leading non-governmental provider of health services on the planet. The history of the Church is replete with saints whose mission was primarily concerned with caring for the ill.

The view that spirituality and religious practices are beneficial to health did not come into question until Sigmund Freud popularized this belief through his writings. Freud, perhaps the most famous psychiatrist of all time, was instrumental in establishing psychiatry as a "medical" science. To do this the soul would be replaced with the "psyche," which could be understood and treated like any other biological organism.

Duke University psychiatrist Harold Koenig details Freud's influence when writing:

> It was not until modern times that religion and psychiatry began to part paths. This separation was encouraged by the psychiatrist Sigmund Freud. After being "introduced" to the neurotic and hysterical aspects of religion by the famous French neurologist Jean Charcot in the mid-1880s, Freud began to emphasize this in a widely read series of publications from 1907 through his death in 1939. Included among these were *Religious Acts and Obsessive Practices*, *Psychoanalysis and Religion* , *Future of an Illusion*, and *Moses and Monotheism* . These writings left a legacy that would influence the practice of psychiatry—especially psychotherapy—for the rest of the century and lead to a true schism between religion and mental health care.[5]

Fortunately, that last twenty years have brought the renewed recognition that religious and spiritual practices are most beneficial to overall health, as well as stress relief in particular.

---

5. Koenig, "Religion, Spirituality, and Health," 2.

APPLICATION

Bracket your day in prayer

The academic literature regarding the benefits of spirituality is well established. Those who regularly partake in spiritual exercise experience a host of mental, emotional, and even physical benefits. Of course, how one practices such activities is highly personal, as there is no "one way" to connect with a higher power.

Yet regardless of which activities we are drawn to, it makes sense to surround ourselves with these disciplines throughout the day. In the Bible there is the assertion to "rejoice always, pray continually, give thanks in all circumstances."[6] Regardless of one's particular religion these are sound ideas to live by.

Humanly speaking it is not practical to literally *pray continually,* since there are other necessary demands at school and work that require our full attention. However, it is possible to surround ourselves in prayer by setting aside time throughout the day for brief prayers, reasons for gratitude, or even simply glances skyward acknowledging our creator, as we understand that being. A simple way to do this is to match the quarter hours on our watch, 6-9-12-3-6-9, with moments to recollect ourselves. At a minimum the recognition of something beyond our *self* helps to bring perspective to our lives and to ease the tension that comes with daily life.

Be spiritual and religious

Spirituality is connection to a higher power through personal activities such as prayer, reading, meditation, yoga, and mindfulness. Religion is the organized grouping of people concerned with spiritual matters. Our culture has placed an emphasis on spirituality at the expense of religion, and this is understandable when looking at the various scandals over the past few decades. But spirituality and religion are two sides of the same coin.

6. 1 Thess 5:16-18.

Spirituality refers to the pursuit of that which brings ultimate meaning and purpose to our lives. Religion simply means belonging to a group that shares an interest in spiritual matters. To practice spirituality without concern or connection with others would seem to miss the mark.

Both individual practices (meditation, yoga, prayer, spending time in nature) *and* communal participation (volunteering, helping others, attending worship services) help us to flourish in this important area of our lives. One does not exclude the other.

Begin (each day) with the end in mind—Purpose!

Perhaps it is fitting to end this manual with this idea of *beginning with the end in mind*. Spiritual truths often present themselves in ways that seem to be paradoxical.

Spirituality and religion, at their core, are connected with one thing we all share as humans: our mortality. Regardless of our race, income, political stance, occupation, or wealth, one day we will all pass from this life to the next. What we come to believe about the afterlife plays a very powerful role in how we live our lives while on this earth.

It is a good idea to spend some time each day thinking about our mortality, and how we choose to spend the time we have. In a consumer culture that tries to drown out this profound reality with never-ending noise, this can be difficult. Social media and marketing now literally bombard us with constant messages that "things" will make us happy. But they don't because they can't. We return to our "normal" sense of happiness shortly after our latest purchase.

There is, of course, nothing wrong with material things. We need them to survive and to enjoy our lives. However, when they begin take the place of our sense of purpose and mission, we can become ruled by them. Daily spiritual practices such as prayer, yoga, and meditation can help us to be better positioned to see much of the minor stressors we face each day for what they are, just little stones along our journey.

STRESS

Simplicity

1. "I'm happiest when I'm out of breath"
2. Listen to your mother!
3. A good night KISS

Exercise

1. Sweat the small stuff
2. Eat chocolate!
3. Double the fun

Think

1. You can't hit what you can't see.
2. The power of *now!*
3. Look for the monster under your bed.

Social

1. You've got to write a letter to get a letter.
2. Book some Face-time with your friends
3. Take your daily medicine

Resilience

1. Run in the rain
2. Live like (weight) lifters
3. Take the long way home

Spiritual

1. Bracket your day in prayers
2. Be *spiritual* and *religious*
3. Begin with the end in mind

Bibliography

"10 Short Parables on Love and Relationship: #3 A Friend You Can't Bear to be Around." http://www.marchantmethod.com/articles/comments/10-short-parables-on-love-relationship.

Axe, Josh. *Eat Dirt: Why Leaky Gut May be the Root Cause of Your Health Problems and 5 Surprising Steps to Cure it.* New York: Harper Wave, 2016.

Barron, Robert. "Religion and the Opening up of the Mind." https://www.wordonfire.org/resources/lecture/religion-and-the-opening-up-of-the-mind-google-talk/5770/.

Blashfield, Roger K., et al. "The Cycle of Classification: DSM I Through DSM 5." *Annual Review of Clinical Psychiatry* 10 (2014) 25–51.

Cannon, Walter B. *Bodily Changes in Pain, Hunger, Fear, and Rage.* New York: D. Appleton, 1929.

Carroll, Andrew, ed. *Letters of a Nation: A Collection of Extraordinary American Letters.* New York: Kodansha, 1990.

Centers for Disease Control and Prevention. "1 in 3 Adults Don't get Enough Sleep." https://www.cdc.gov/media/releases/2016/p0215-enough-sleep.html.

———. "Obesity and Overweight". https://www.cdc.gov/nchs/fastats/obesity-overweight.htm.

Chesterton, G.K. *All Things Considered.* London: Methuan, 1908.

———. *More Quotable Chesterton: A Topical Compilation of the Wit, Wisdom and Satire of G.K. Chesterton.* Edited by George J. Marlin, Richard P. Rabatin, and John L. Swan. San Francisco: Ignatius Press, 1988.

"Christmas Truce of 1914." https://www.history.com/topics/world-war-i/christmas-truce-of-1914.

Cohen, Hiyaguha. "Americans Spend More Eating Out Than at Home." Baseline of Health Foundation. https://jonbarron.org/diet-and-nutrition/americans-spend-more-eating-out-home.

Conrad, Peter. *The Medicalization of Society.* Baltimore: Johns Hopkins, 2007.

"Dr. Carl Jung's letter to Bill W., Jan. 30, 1961." https://silkworth.net/pages/aahistory/general/carljung_billwo13061.php.

Engel, George L. "The Need for a New Medical Model: A Challenge for Biomedicine." *Family Systems Medicine* 10 (1992) 317–31.

Freedhoff, Yoni, and Arya M. Sharma. ""Lose 40 Pounds in 4 Weeks": Regulating Commercial Weight-Loss Program." *Canadian Medical Association Journal* 180 (2009) 367.

Goldman, Stuart. "Jack LaLanne Leads Others to Fitness." https://www.clubindustry. com/forprofits/jack-lalanne-leads-others-fitness.

"Good Luck? Bad Luck? Who Knows?" http://www.ribessj.org/GOOD_LUCK_ BAD_LUCK_WHO_KNOWS.pdf.

"In the Womb Two Babies Debate Matters of Fact and Faith." https://aleteia. org/2017/01/26/in the womb two babies debate-matters-of-facts-and-faith/.

Koenig, Harold G. "Religion, Spirituality, and Health: The Research and Clinical Implications." *International Scholarly Research Network* (2012) 1–33. https://pdfs.semanticscholar.org/a35b/e2420b131c0aa034bea06d20f2a2 543c8c72.pdf.

"Lessons from a Greek Fisherman." https://www.bluemts.com.au/businessinfo. asp?pid=65&bid=20&id=76.

Louv, Richard. "Do Our Kids Have Nature-Deficit Disorder?" *Educational Leadership* 67 (2009) 24–30.

Lyubomirsky, Sonya. *The How of Happiness: A Scientific Approach to Getting the Life You Want.* New York: Penguin, 2007.

MacLoad, Elizabeth, et al. *A History of Just About Everything: 180 Events, People and Inventions that Changed the World.* Toronto: Kids Can, 2013.

McKinlay, John B. "A Case for Refocusing Upstream." In *Sociology of Health and Illness: Critical Perspectives,* edited by Peter Conrad and Rochelle Kern, 502–16. New York: St. Martins Press, 1990.

Miller, Douglas T., and Nowak, Marion. *The Fifties: The Way We Really Were.* New York: Doubleday, 1977.

"On the Medicalization of Our Culture." https://harvardmagazine.com/2009/04/ medicalization-of-our-culture.

Samani, Ashna, and Heath, Matthew. "Executive-related oculomotor control is improved following a 10-minute single-bout of aerobic exercise: Evidence from the antisaccade task." *Neuropsychologia* 108 (2018) 73–81.

Seligman, Martin E.P. *Authentic Happiness: Using the New Positive Psychology to Realize Your Potential for Lasting Fulfillment.* New York: Free, 2002.

Selye, Hans. *The Stress of My Life: A Scientist's Memoirs.* New York: Van Nostrand Reinhold, 1979.

Shakya, Holly, and Christakis, Nickolas. "A new more rigorous study confirms, the more you use Facebook, the worse you feel." *Harvard Business Review.* (2017). https://hbr.org/2017/04/a-new-more-rigorous-study-confirms-the- more-you-use-facebook-the-worse-you-feel.

Twenge, Jean M., et al. "Birth Cohort Increases in Psychopathology Among Young Americans, 1938–2007: A Cross-Temporal Meta-Analysis of the MMPI." *Clinical Psychology Review* 30 (2010) 145–54.

"The Two Wolves." http://www.nanticokeindians.org/page/tale-of-two-wolves.

US Food and Drug Administration. "Beware of Products Promising Miracle Weight Loss." https://www.fda.gov/ForConsumers/ConsumerUpdates/ucm246742.htm.

Umberson, Debra, and Montez, Jennifer Karas. "Social Relationships and Health: A Flashpoint for Health Policy." *Journal of Health and Social Behavior* 51 (2010) 54–66. http://www.ncbi.nlm.nih.gov/pmc/articles/PMC3150158/.

University of Western Ontario. "Short-term exercise equals big-time brain boost: Even a one-time, brief burst of exercise can improve focus, problem-solving." *ScienceDaily.* www.sciencedaily.com/releases/2017/12/171221122543.htm

Weitz, Rose. *The Sociology of Health, Illness, and Health Care: A Critical Approach.* Boston: Wadsworth, 2015.

Wilson, Bill. *Alcoholics Anonymous Comes of Age: A Brief History of A.A.* New York: Alcoholics Anonymous, 1957.

Yogman, Michael, et al. "The Power of Play: A Pediatric Role in Enhancing Development in Young Children." *American Academy of Pediatrics* 142 (2018) 1–16.

Yorks, Dayna M., et al. "Effects of Group Fitness Classes on Stress and Quality of Life of Medical Students." *The Journal of the American Osteopathic Association* 117 (2017) e17-e25. http://jaoa.org/article.aspx?articleid=2661140.

Made in the USA
Middletown, DE
24 March 2019